BTS K-POP KINGS

Portable Press
An imprint of Printers Row Publishing Group
10350 Barnes Canyon Road, Suite 100, San Diego, CA 92121
www.portablepress.com • mail@portablepress.com

Correspondence regarding the contents of this book should be addressed to Portable Press, Editorial Department, at the above address. Author or image inquiries should be addressed to Michael O'Mara Books Limited, 9 Lion Yard, Tremadoc Road, London, SW4 7NQ, Great Britain, www.mombooks.com.

This book is not affiliated with or endorsed by BTS or any of their publishers or licensees.

Portable Press
Publisher: Peter Norton
Associate Publisher: Ana Parker
Senior Developmental Editor: April Graham Farr
Senior Product Manager: Kathryn C. Dalby
Production Team: Jonathan Lopes, Rusty von Dyl

Michael O'Mara Books
Editors: Helen Brown and Hannah Daffern
Designer: Derrian Bradder
Cover design: Angie Allison

Author: Helen Brown

Library of Congress Cataloging-in-Publication Data is available upon request.

ISBN: 978-1-64517-137-9

Printed in China

23 22 21 20 19   1 2 3 4 5

Picture Credits:

BTS K-POP KINGS

PORTABLE
PRESS

San Diego, California

CONTENTS

CHAPTER ONE:
The Beginnings of K-pop

Before BTS burst on to the scene, Korean pop was on the rise and growing in popularity around the world. So where did it all begin?

When BTS became the first **K-pop** act to top the US Billboard album charts in 2018, many people were asking who this band were and where they had come from. Had you ever seen anything like BTS before? The perfectly choreographed moves? Both rappers and singers in the same group? The slick looks and edgy style? They were seen as an overnight sensation, but as any true fan will know, BTS have dedicated themselves to ground-breaking K-pop for years. They've worked incredibly hard to become a global phenomenon.

K-pop began with Seo Taiji and Boys, a South Korean band who performed on MBC network's weekly talent show on April 11, 1992. Before this point, South Korea's travel ban and strict censorship laws meant that the usual styles of K-pop were traditional "trot" (short for "foxtrot") and ballads. Seo Taiji and Boys's performance of the rap-rock break-up song "Nan Arayo" ("I Know") was pioneering – the trendy American rap fused with Korean lyrics had never been seen before.

Despite receiving the lowest votes from the judges for their performance on MBC, people were clearly ready for change as the song topped the country's charts for 17 weeks. It marked the beginning of the remarkable K-pop scene known today.

By the time Seo Taiji and Boys disbanded in 1996, they had inspired a generation of performers who were eager to experiment with many different genres of popular western music and give them a unique Korean twist.

RISE UP

Music studios dedicated to K-pop started to appear and, over the next few years, three powerhouse music companies began a process that produced successful artists and groups who would become known as "idol groups."

To this day, these companies host extremely competitive auditions in search of talent.

QUICK QUESTION
Which are the biggest three K-pop companies in South Korea?

Answer: SM Entertainment, JYP Entertainment, YG Entertainment

The performers start early — some audition as young as nine years old. The auditions focus on five categories: vocal, dance, acting, modeling and writing/composing music.

If successful, the young artists selected become known as **trainees**. They live together in a dorm and often work 14-hour days. Alongside their school curriculum, they undertake a demanding boot camp of singing, dancing, exercise and language lessons (mostly English and Japanese) as well as learning how to act like a superstar in front of the camera.

The soon-to-be stars are put together to build a perfect combination of performers and personalities. K-pop groups strive to achieve a complete package of skills — they have specialist rappers, vocalists, dancers and even members who are included just for their looks! The training period for K-pop stars can last years as there is so much to learn before they are officially unveiled to the world.

THE DEBUT

The K-pop agencies work around the clock to put out teaser videos and photographs, set up social media accounts and start fan clubs months before the group is launched on stage. The enthusiasm of K-pop fans plays a crucial part in the success of a band, so this early interaction gives the chance to build anticipation and excitement for their debut.

Awareness of K-pop and Korean culture is growing globally. This is known as **hallyu**. There's worldwide interest from Japan to the US, and BTS's domination as the K-pop kings shows no sign of slowing down. They are conquering the world.

♥ ♥ ♥ ♥ ♥ ♥ ♥

K-pop is commonly classified as "popular music" within South Korea. The term is used to describe a modern form of South Korean pop music that is influenced by styles and genres from around the world.

♥ ♥ ♥ ♥ ♥ ♥ ♥

Trainees are young performers signed to an entertainment company in order to train in dance, singing and study other performing acts with a view to becoming an idol.

♥ ♥ ♥ ♥ ♥ ♥ ♥

Hallyu means the "Korean Wave," and refers to the growing interest in South Korean culture around the world in the 21st century.

♥ ♥ ♥ ♥ ♥ ♥ ♥

★ ★ ★ ★ ★ ★ ★

DID YOU KNOW?

In 2017, Seo Taiji and Boys held a 25th anniversary concert where they collaborated with K-pop group of the moment BTS.

★ ★ ★ ★ ★ ★ ★

CHAPTER TWO:
Coming Together

BTS came together after years of hard work, dedication and a huge amount of talent. Follow in their footsteps and discover their journey to stardom.

BTS began with one man – Bang Si-hyuk. Bang Si-hyuk had a successful career working as a composer and producer with JYP Entertainment but in 2005 decided to set up his own company called Big Hit Entertainment. His aim was to create a company that nurtured its performing artists and one where the trainees' styles and personalities could radiate. Bang Si-hyuk worked with other K-pop groups over the next five years, but it wasn't until 2010 that he had the idea to launch a hip-hop idol group.

"I thought that the group shouldn't just be idols who do hip-hop, but rather members who can tell their own stories. This thought has consistently been reflected in BTS's music and has not changed now either."
– Bang Si-hyuk in 2016

The hard work began to make an idea become a reality. Kim Namjoon (RM) had joined Big Hit in 2010, after being scouted as a rapper in the underground scene. Jung Hoseok (J-Hope) was next to join the ranks as an amazing dancer and singer, and later became a rapper.

CHANGE OF PLAN

It soon became clear to Bang Si-hyuk that rapping alone wasn't mainstream enough for these boys to take the world by storm. So, the hunt began for a less rap-focused group, with a sprinkling of vocalists mixed in.

In early 2012, Jeon Jungkook (Jungkook), Kim Taehyung (V) and Kim Seokjin (Jin) joined the team as singers. Perfection was brewing. By the summer of 2012, Park Jimin (Jimin) signed up and the idol group was ready.

The line-up changed over the two years of training, but the final seven members were a dynamite mix of talent, drive, personality and looks. They were willing to put in hours of hard work and had potential. A few different names floated around – from "Big Kids" to "Young Nation" – but they wanted a name that conveyed their message. Bang Si-hyuk finally came up with the perfect name: **Bangtan Sonyeondan**, or **BTS**.

ALSO KNOWN AS:

BANGTAN BOYS
BULLETPROOF BOYSCOUTS
BODAN SHONENDAN
BEYOND THE SCENE

★ ★ ★ ★ ★ ★ ★

DID YOU KNOW?

RM has worked with other underground rappers, including Kidoh who ended up in idol group Topp Dogg.

★ ★ ★ ★ ★ ★ ★

RM
rapper, producer, leader

Jin
vocalist, visual

Suga
rapper, producer

J-Hope
rapper, dancer

Jimin
vocalist, dancer

V
vocalist, visual

Jungkook
vocalist, dancer, **maknae**

♥ ♥ ♥ ♥ ♥ ♥ ♥

Bangtan translates as "bulletproof."

♥ ♥ ♥ ♥ ♥ ♥ ♥

Sonyeondan means a group
of boys or boy scouts.

♥ ♥ ♥ ♥ ♥ ♥ ♥

Maknae is the term given to the
youngest member of a K-pop group.

♥ ♥ ♥ ♥ ♥ ♥ ♥

**"The meaning of 'bangtan' is to guard
against something ... We will boldly
defend our music and our values."**

– J-Hope in 2015

Bangtan Sonyeondan became both the name and the identity of the group. It showed the world that they would speak out for all their fans and fight against the injustices faced by their generation. Through their lyrics, they speak freely about mental health and the importance of self worth. They take on the responsibility of helping fans overcome hardships and encourage fans to speak up with them. They communicate directly to fans through a range of social media channels and have created a tight bond that gets stronger every year.

> **"We came together with a common dream to write, dance, and produce music that reflects our musical backgrounds as well as our life values of acceptance, vulnerability and being successful."**
> — RM in 2017

READY TO LAUNCH

Back in 2012, a blog announced the pending arrival of Bangtan Sonyeondan (BTS), including photos of the boys and teasers to excite early followers. The word was out – BTS were the new idol group in town.

Before their official debut, the boys had released videos to their fans through YouTube. On December 17, 2012, RM uploaded the first video of him doing a cover of "Power" by Kanye West.

★ ★ ★ ★ ★ ★

DID YOU KNOW?

BTS's YouTube channel "BANGTANTV" currently has over 14 million subscribers worldwide.

During this time, the boys recorded video blogs and talked to fans directly. They made solo videos and discussed a range of topics, from J-Hope's hopes for the group to more serious anxieties like Jungkook's homesickness. The videos were honest and sensitive, but also funny and silly. They showed the qualities that fans would later come to love about BTS.

TIME TO DEBUT

It wasn't until May 21, 2013, when a countdown-to-debut clock appeared along with a trailer, that things started to feel real. Their official debut video was a black-and-white montage of the members' names, including the slogan "the exclusive fight against prejudice." It finished with "BTS" emblazoned on a bullet-proof vest. Fans did not have to wait long for the countdown to be over – 22 days later, BTS made their debut showcase. It took place on June 12 at the Gangnam Ilchi Art Hall in Cheongdam-dong, Seoul. Wearing all black, with gold chains, sunglasses and lots of leather, the boys had all the hallmarks of a cool boy band. When asked which bands they looked up to, RM said, "BIG BANG [a rival South Korean boy band formed by YG Entertainment] is at the top as hip-hop idols, so we're learning from them."

But the next day was the one that counted. The boys finally appeared live on stage for the first time on South Korean TV shows *M Countdown* and *Music Bank*. They performed two songs: "No More Dream" and "We Are Bulletproof Pt. 2." The crowds went wild.

It was an epic performance that matched their swagger – they radiated confidence and had the dance moves and rap skills to match. Every move and sound was perfectly in sync and all seven members made a unique contribution. This distinctiveness was there from the beginning and is still in the band to this day.

DID YOU KNOW?

BTS set up a group on the internet forum "fan-café" which had 55,000 members after their debut performance. It currently has over 1.5 million members.

★ ★ ★ ★ ★ ★

The boys have evolved since the group's debut. In July 2017, the group extended their identity with a new name: **BEYOND THE SCENE**.

A short video was released showing two new logos, one for BTS and one for the fans. RM signed off the video by saying, "Beyond the scene, BTS".

"More than anything, the new identity shows that [our fans] and we, BTS, are connected as one and are filled with meaning that makes us feel good."
– Twitter (@BTS_twt) in 2017

QUICK QUESTION

In July 2017, BTS released a video displaying the two new logos, one for BTS and one for the fans. What three colors are used?

Answer: Black, white, gray

RM

Name:
Kim Namjoon

Also known as:
RM, Rap Monster, Dance Prodigy,
God of Destruction

Date of birth:
September 12, 1994

Star sign:
Virgo

Birthplace:
Ilsan, South Korea

Height:
5'11"

Education:
Apgujeong High School,
Global Cyber University

Languages:
Korean, English, Japanese

Early career:
Breakout in 2008 as Runch Randa

Joined BTS:
2010 as the first member

RM grew up watching videos of American rappers and became a renowned rapper on the underground scene before being selected as the first member of BTS in 2010.

"I loved writing lyrics for rap when I was in junior high. I loved studying, but somehow I wanted to be a rapper who can write and rap."

RM is the leader of BTS and the driving force for the band, charging them with the responsibility of being better than the average idol group. RM has written some of the band's most powerful songs, from their debut "No More Dream" to "Spine Breaker."

"My songs have made me someone who constantly observes society and wants to be a person who can have [a] better, positive impact on other people."

RM speaks flawless English and is the voice of the group when interviewed in the US and the UK. He even knows colloquial slang and has a great sense of humor.

RM taught himself how to speak and understand English by watching the American TV show *Friends*. He watched all ten seasons three times – first with Korean subtitles, then with English subtitles, and lastly with no subtitles. He admitted to *Elle* magazine in 2017 that he most liked the character Chandler, as he had always admired his sense of humor.

It's no surprise that RM picked up English so quickly – he has an IQ of 148, which is in the top 2% of Korea. He excelled in Korean language, math and foreign languages at school and his parents and teachers were keen for him to continue studying. But RM had other ideas. He followed his dreams, and when he passed his audition at Big Hit Entertainment in 2010, he never looked back.

RM spent three years training, but although rapping came naturally to him, he struggled with dancing. He continues to work to become a better dancer as he feels like a nuisance to the other members in the group.

RM can be sensitive about comments that are written online. He once confessed that he had spent five days thinking about a comment that took someone five seconds to write. The most hurtful comment he ever read was one pressuring him to leave the group. He found it hard not to listen to the voices of others but knew deep down that they were wrong.

"I have many faults, and I have many more fears, but I'm gonna embrace myself as hard as I can, and I'm starting to love myself gradually, just little by little."

RM's interests extend beyond music. He enjoys reading Japanese authors, such as Banana Yoshimoto and Haruki Murakami, and has a soft-spot for love stories, including Jojo Moyes's *Me Before You*. It's clear that this passion for literature feeds into his song writing. The giant Omelas sign in the video for "Spring Day" recalls Ursula K. Le Guin's short story *The Ones Who Walk Away from Omelas*.

Although RM is the group's leader, he is not its eldest member. This is a little unusual for a K-pop group, because in Korean society age is very important. But RM was the first member of BTS and his ideas contributed to the direction of the group, so he was appointed as the leader. It's important to RM that the group has a positive attitude and all the members feel equally valued. Like a true leader, RM always puts the other members before himself. When Bang Si-hyuk asked him to choose between a solo career or BTS, he answered "BTS" without hesitating.

Until 2017, RM was known as "Rap Monster," but changed his name to RM because he felt it was too aggressive. This didn't come as much of a surprise to fans, as other members have let it slip that RM's stage persona isn't the real RM. The boys have also spilled that RM is the clumsiest member of the group and breaks everything he touches. It gets so bad that they've nicknamed him the God of Destruction!

STYLE FILE

Along with being the tallest, RM is arguably one of the most stylish members of the group. He posts regular pictures of himself on BTS's official Twitter account. He loves black clothing and puts pieces together effortlessly.

Although there's an emphasis on black and white, he mixes this up with 70s denim. He's often seen wearing this jacket opposite with shorts to give off a school-boy vibe. He's rarely without a comfy black beanie and dark sunglasses, which finishes off his chic look.

♥ ♥ ♥ ♥ ♥ ♥ ♥

What do the boys say about RM?

Suga:
"RM wears sunglasses and has a powerful image, but he actually likes cute things."

Jungkook:
"He eats other people's food without telling them."

QUICK QUESTION
When Jin was speaking to *Haru Hana* magazine, what did he call RM?

Answer: The Baby Dinosaur Dolly because RM shakes his tail and crushes things

CHAPTER THREE:
ARMY

BTS have hundreds of thousands of supporters who are the most dedicated fans in the world. Check out all the amazing things they have done for their favorite boy band.

"I would like to attribute the glory to all of our ARMYs. I think that even if you make music you need people to listen to it in order to climb up. I'm always grateful to ARMYs and love them."

– Jin, after entering the Billboard Hot 100 for the first time in 2017

On July 9, 2013, BTS announced the name of their official fan club: **ARMY**. And ever since, ARMY have found incredible ways to support and represent the band.

♥ ♥ ♥ ♥ ♥ ♥ ♥

ARMY is the official name given to BTS fans. It's an acronym for "Adorable Representative MC for Youth." It describes the army of fans devoted to spreading the music of BTS and messages of love and acceptance.

♥ ♥ ♥ ♥ ♥ ♥ ♥

The passion of the fans has been the driving force behind BTS's rise — ARMY create an online buzz and hype so loud that it cannot be ignored. They have propelled BTS into the spotlight through their devotion and have created a whole new space for **fandom**.

♥ ♥ ♥ ♥ ♥ ♥ ♥

Fandom is short for "fan domain" and it includes everything that goes on in the fan community, including fan clubs and online forums.

♥ ♥ ♥ ♥ ♥ ♥ ♥

BTS sing and conduct interviews almost entirely in Korean, so ARMY spend their time translating lyrics and interviews for others. They spread the word of BTS far and wide across the internet. Their platform is used to fuel campaigns and to boost sales. They lobby radio stations to play BTS tracks, and they vote for BTS in both TV music shows and top national and international awards.

★ ★ ★ ★ ★ ★ ★

DID YOU KNOW?

In May 2016, BTS were the first K-pop group to earn their own Twitter emoji. The emoji mirrored their bulletproof-vest logo, which was a reference to their Korean name, Bangtan Sonyeondan.

★ ★ ★ ★ ★ ★ ★

TWITTER MANIA

ARMY rallied clicks, views, likes and retweets to get BTS trending on Twitter. Their efforts paid off when BTS became the most retweeted Twitter account in 2017. BTS were further recognized when they received a Guinness World Record as the music act with the most Twitter engagement after they generated 51.72 million tweets for one hashtag.

DEVOTION

The boys acknowledge the significance of their fan base. There is a tight symbiosis between ARMY and BTS. Along with their constant interaction on social media, BTS make sure they give back to their fans during their concerts. They performed on stages around the world through 2018 and 2019, and showcased both old favorite tunes and new songs, never-seen-before videos and epic stage costumes. They engaged with their audience, and in turn the fans gave love back through a beautiful display of light sticks, banners and chants. The most common fan chant is one that calls out the names of the members. It is important to get the correct order for the chant: "Kim Namjoon! Kim Seokjin! Min Yoongi! Jung Hoseok! Park Jimin! Kim Taehyung! Jeon Jungkook! BTS!"

SOCIAL CAUSES

In 2018, ARMY participated in a campaign where every time the hashtag #RoarForChange was used on social media, the organization Star Wars: Force for Change pledged to donate one US dollar to support UNICEF. As UNICEF was BTS's chosen charity, ARMY were enlisted, and in a couple of hours they had gathered enough tweets to help raise 1 million dollars.

The help extends to each other through unofficial groups such as The Army Help Centre who are a team of ARMYs from all around the world who volunteer their time to help other fans. They use the hashtag #SpreadLovePositivity to connect with people when they need emotional help or support. Although they are not affiliated with BTS or Big Hit Entertainment, they have created a family. They reach out to both young and old and express the true importance of loving others and loving yourself.

It's easy to get lost in BTS's music, their moves and their records, but one of BTS's greatest achievements is how they have brought people together over the years. They have created and nurtured a fan base that spans the world through different cultures and generations, who embrace not only love for the band, but for one another.

QUICK QUESTION

A BTS Twitter emoji was used to track fans across the world for a global contest. Which five countries had the highest number of tweets and each received a special video message from the boys?

Answer: Brazil, Turkey, Russia, Thailand , South Korea

Follow the official accounts to stay up to date with all things BTS.

Website
♥ bts.ibighit.com ♥
The official website featuring all the music videos, tour information, concept photos and much more.

Blog
♥ btsblog.ibighit.com ♥
The official blog on the history of BTS and their music.

Twitter
♥ @BTS_twt ♥
The boys post updates from their shared handle.
♥ @bts_bighit ♥
The official account run by Big Hit Entertainment.

YouTube
♥ BANGTANTV ♥
Short videos of behind-the-scenes footage, as well as music videos and dance practice videos.

Instagram
♥ @bts.bighitofficial ♥
The official account for concept photos, teaser videos and messages from the group.

Facebook
♥ bangtan.official ♥
The official account for sharing posts and connecting with the group and the community.

Forums
♥ cafe.daum.net/BANGTAN ♥
The forum to communicate with fans and encourage discussion.

JIN

Name:
Kim Seokjin

Also known as:
Jin, Worldwide Handsome,
Visual King, Granny

Date of birth:
December 4, 1992

Star sign:
Sagittarius

Birthplace:
Anyang, Gyeonggi Province,
South Korea

Height:
5'10"

Education:
Bosung High School,
Konkuk University,
Global Cyber University

Languages:
Korean, English, Japanese,
basic Mandarin Chinese

Early career:
Degree in art and acting

Joined BTS:
2012

Jin studied acting at the Department of Film and Visual Arts at Konkuk University. He had only been at university for three months when he was scouted and asked to audition for Big Hit Entertainment. Jin originally auditioned as an actor and became the first non-rapper to join BTS.

"Looking back at my audition, I didn't know anything – what to do or how to sing."

Jin is considered the best-looking in the group. His broad shoulders and handsome features attract a lot of attention. It was his looks that originally brought him to BTS when Big Hit Entertainment selected him in a street cast. Rumor has it that a casting director chased Jin as he got off a bus because he was so good-looking!

"I think I'm Worldwide Handsome."

Education is important to Jin, so he continued to study and graduated in 2017. He wasn't able to attend his graduation because the group were at an awards ceremony, so BTS celebrated his graduation with fans over a live show.

Jin once described his childhood as "idyllic" – with extravagant skiing and golfing vacations. Now an adult, he is still very close to his family, especially his mother. The boys have commented that he can stay on the phone to her for over an hour. Once he made a Valentine's Day present for his mom, although it didn't go to plan – he melted a lot of chocolate together and burned it!

As the biggest foodie in the group, Jin cannot get enough of cooking, eating and talking about food. He created a blog named "Jin's Recipes" to show how dull the trainee food was. In 2015 he began a VLIVE series called *Eat Jin*; his own **mukbang**, which has had two seasons so far. In the first season, Jin ate large quantities of food and in the second season he ate while interacting with ARMY via livestream. The most popular episode was when he attempted to consume an entire **jjajangmyeon** in one minute!

The BTS boys have a close relationship because they live together. Jin is in charge of the kitchen and often finds himself cleaning and tidying. He has commented on the other boys just dumping groceries anywhere in the kitchen, whereas he always puts all the groceries in the fridge and makes sure he throws away the rotten food. His kitchen skills served him well when in July 2018 he opened a restaurant with his older brother specializing in Japanese dishes. Jimin is apparently already a very loyal customer.

In the dorm, Jin takes on a parental role as he rises two hours before the others. He likes to make sure that they are awake and he likes to cook for the group. It's no surprise that he's earned the nickname "Granny"!

The man with the nickname "Worldwide Handsome" also likes to spend his time perfecting his good looks. He is known as the "visual" of the group which means he's seen as the best-looking member of BTS.

"Skin is what completes my appearance. I value my looks very much, so it's equally important to take good care of my skin."

Jin is also the oldest member of the band and serves as a vocalist. He had little music experience before joining and after their debut, Jin received criticism. Some people called him the "black hole of dancing." He had to work very hard to hone the singing and dancing skills he is now known for. He still remains modest about his dancing – in 2017 he told a TV show, "I think I am really bad at dancing." But he cheekily added, "however, Rap Monster really cannot dance!"

"At first it was really hard but there were lots of kids who helped me and treated me really well. They helped me a lot and said things like 'try listening to this song,' 'try doing it this way,' and so training became easier."

♥　♥　♥　♥　♥　♥　♥

Mukbang is a livestream or video where people film themselves eating large quantities of food.

♥　♥　♥　♥　♥　♥

Jjajangmyeon is a popular dish of noodles in black bean sauce.

♥　♥　♥　♥　♥　♥

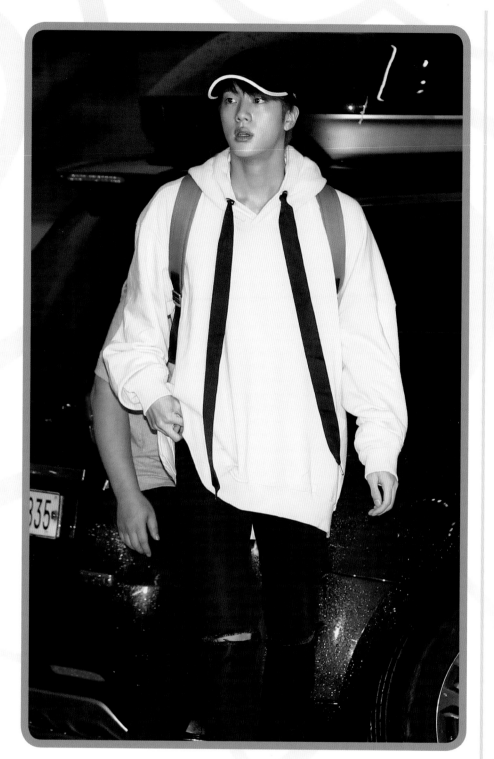

STYLE FILE

Jin always dresses to make an impression. His outfits require a lot of thought and often include an accessory such as a hat to complete the look. Jin pulls off any style of hat – from a beanie to a baseball cap – but it is a shame that it covers his gorgeous face! Whether it's a pair of glasses, a hat or an oversized coat, his style is clean cut and stylish. He loves the color pink and if his hair isn't pink then his T-shirt or sweater definitely will be.

What do the boys say about Jin?

V:
"He's a prince."

Jungkook:
"He's a good cook, so we all call him 'Granny'!"

QUICK QUESTION

After "Granny," what is Jin's most popular nickname?

CHAPTER FOUR:
Journey Through Music

BTS have released many albums since their debut in 2013. From hip-hop to dance music, the band show that they can do any genre.

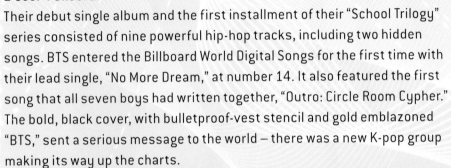

2 Cool 4 Skool EP

June 13, 2013

Their debut single album and the first installment of their "School Trilogy" series consisted of nine powerful hip-hop tracks, including two hidden songs. BTS entered the Billboard World Digital Songs for the first time with their lead single, "No More Dream," at number 14. It also featured the first song that all seven boys had written together, "Outro: Circle Room Cypher." The bold, black cover, with bulletproof-vest stencil and gold emblazoned "BTS," sent a serious message to the world – there was a new K-pop group making its way up the charts.

O!RUL8,2? EP

September 11, 2013

A few months later, their first mini-album was released as part two of the "School Trilogy" series. This ten-track album featured "N.O" (also known as "No Offense") as the lead single. The music video featured the boys in a dystopian school where students are uniformed and taken to lessons under armed guard. Jungkook starts a rebellion – leading the boys from the school to a bright, white studio. The video celebrated a new concept as BTS ditched the bold, black look for an angelic white, with the cover album to match.

Skool Luv Affair EP

February 12, 2014

The second mini-album and the third installment of the "School Trilogy" series was released the following year around Valentine's Day. This ten-track album marked their first comeback in that year and they promoted "Boy in Luv" as the title track. The series concept showed the group as the school bad boys, tough and wild but with gentle hearts capable of young love. The metallic pink lettering on the cover shows this loving side. The world was beginning to warm to BTS, as the album went to number one in the Korean chart and number three in the Billboard World Albums Chart.

Dark & Wild   August 19, 2014

Later that year, BTS released their 14-track, full-length debut album. The concept photos and album cover revealed a more mature look that matched the grown-up tone of the songs. The bad-boy image was still there, and there was a dark feel from the video for their lead track, "Danger," but they had moved away from school and focused on love. The glossy, dark-black background with white scratch marks felt eerie, along with the red-and-white "WARNING!" message: "LOVE HURTS, IT CAUSES ANGER, JEALOUSY, OBSESSION. WHY DON'T U LOVE ME BACK?"

The Most Beautiful Moment in Life Pt. 1 EP   April 29, 2015

BTS kicked off in 2015 with their third mini-album which reflected on the realities of life. They left their brooding thoughts behind as they cherished the moments of joy and beauty in growing up. This nine-track album was not only successful in South Korea, but topped music charts in Japan, China and the US with beautiful tracks such as "I Need U." They released two album designs for this EP, one pink and the other white, to reflect a change in direction and a new era for the band.

The Most Beautiful Moment in Life Pt. 2 EP   November 30, 2015

The concept flowed through the year into part two with a peach version or a blue version for the choice of cover designs. This fourth mini-album contained nine tracks, with "Run" as the lead. The album showcased a new, rich pop sound, which brought the rappers and the vocal line closer again, proving to the world that BTS had come a long way in such a short time. They embarked on a huge world tour as this EP topped a record-setting six international music charts, including Billboard's World Album Charts. After four weeks, they set a record as the first K-pop act to achieve this.

The Most Beautiful Moment in Life: Young Forever   May 2, 2016

This special compilation album was the last of *The Most Beautiful Moment in Life* series. It featured 23 tracks, including tracks from *Pt. 1* and *Pt. 2*, a few remixes and three new tracks, "Fire," "Save Me" and "Epilogue: Young Forever." The album won the "Album of the Year" award at the Melon Music Awards. The cover depicts a multi-colored hot-air balloon carrying the boys up high into the skies.

Wings   October 10, 2016

This 15-track, second full album showed BTS embracing a more mature, elegant look in their crisp dress shirts and floral jackets. The dramatic video for "Blood, Sweat & Tears" displayed their innocence being left behind and their alluring appeal taking the spotlight. It gave the fans exactly what they were looking for, and the video reached more than 6 million views in under 24 hours. The album debuted in the top 30 of the Billboard 200 and BTS became the first K-pop band with three albums to enter the main album charts. The second song on the album, "Blood, Sweat & Tears," achieved an "all-kill" as it hit No. 1 on all eight Korean charts at the same time. The album created scope for creative growth for the band as it featured seven solo tracks that showcased the personality of each member.

You Never Walk Alone   February 13, 2017

BTS re-released *Wings* four months later as *You Never Walk Alone*, featuring four new songs, including "Not Today" and "Spring Day." These new tracks were all written by members of the group as messages of hope. The group posed in front of the sea in colorful casual wear, and this theme of hopefulness continued through to the video for "Spring Day" with dreamy pastel colors.

Love Yourself: Her EP

September 18, 2017

The fifth mini-album appeared in four versions, *L*, *O*, *V* and *E*. The concept photos for the first two versions are gentle, contrasting with the second two versions which are vibrant. They are tied together through a feeling of genuine happiness and a zest for life. The lead track "DNA" exuded exactly that, with an upbeat melody and a focus on the group's epic dance moves. The song "Best of Me" featured a collaboration between BTS and the American DJ/production duo The Chainsmokers. It was a hit and it became the first K-pop album to debut in the Billboard 200 top ten when it entered the chart at number seven.

Love Yourself: Tear

May 18, 2018

Once again, this 11-track third full album had four versions, *Y*, *O*, *U* and *R*. Stylish and yearning, this album was dripping with the joy and pain of love and loss. The dark tunes echo the black cover which had intricate line art. The lead single "Fake Love" explored the complex feelings of love and it made K-pop history when it entered the Billboard 200 top ten in June 2018. It also became BTS's highest-charting single to date in the US.

Love Yourself: Answer

August 24, 2018

A mere three months later, this compilation album brought together tracks from *Her* and *Tear*, along with seven new songs. The main track on this album was "Idol"; the digital album included a version of "Idol" featuring Nicki Minaj. It became BTS's first song to reach the top 40 of the UK's Official Singles chart, ranking at number 21. The album had a powerful theme running through it that everyone has their own path to self-acceptance.

SUGA

Name:
Min Yoongi

Also known as:
Suga, Motionless Min,
Agust D, Grandpa

Date of birth:
March 9, 1993

Star sign:
Pisces

Birthplace:
Daegu, South Korea

Height:
5'9"

Education:
Daegu Taejeon Elementary School,
Gwaneum Middle School,
Kangbuk High School,
Apgujeong High School,
Global Cyber University

Languages:
Korean, basic English,
basic Japanese

Early career:
Underground rapper
named Gloss in D-Town

Joined BTS:
2010, originally joined
as a producer

Suga grew up in Daegu, South Korea, and had a harder upbringing than most of the other boys as his family did not have much money. After debuting, Suga admitted that he couldn't believe that a poor child from Daegu could come so far.

"I came back to our dorm, sat [down] for a long time and stared at nothingness. I couldn't believe that a child that grew in poverty could make his dream come true."

As a teenager, Suga taught himself how to operate music production software and worked part time at a recording studio. He learned how to compose and arrange songs, along with writing lyrics.

"I have been writing rhymes and lyrics, a habit since I was a kid. They are all the little minor feelings and thoughts that go through my mind. I shuffle them a year or so later, and they sometimes become great lyrics for songs."

He began to make a name for himself in the Daegu music scene as he became a dependable source for "beats" (backing tracks) and producing mixtapes. Before being signed to BTS, Suga was known as an underground rapper under the name Gloss and was a member of hip-hop crew D-Town.

When Suga turned 18, he spotted a flyer announcing that Bang Si-hyuk was holding auditions for aspiring rappers. He passed the initial round, but only came second in the final rap battle. It was hugely disappointing, but luckily Bang Si-hyuk had been impressed by Suga's talent and invited him to join Big Hit Entertainment as a trainee. After RM, he became the second member to join BTS.

Now a trainee, Suga needed an idol name. He wanted to keep his original rapper name "Gloss" but was advised to choose something different. Bang Si-hyuk came up with the name Suga which was an immediate hit. He is as sweet and pale as sugar, and it also refers to his postion on the basketball court: shooting guard.

Suga's parents were not happy with his decision to follow a career in music. It was his older brother who supported him from the beginning. But once his parents saw how passionate he was about music, they changed their minds and became enthusiastic fans. They have attended many BTS events over the years and it means the world to Suga to have their support. Suga's parents were in the crowd at BTS's 2016 The Most Beautiful Moment in Life: Epilogue concert. When Suga saw them, he fell to his knees, bowed to them and started to cry.

Suga found a second family in BTS and has a special bond with all of the boys. He shared a room with Jin until the most recent move and believes him to be the perfect roommate. When asked if he would ever consider swapping, he replied with a firm "Never." He has a special role in the group as he's the one the boys turn to when they need advice. The boys call Suga "Grandpa" because of his wise personality, the fact he fixes everything around the house, and because he loves to nap.

In January 2018, Suga was promoted to a full member of the Korea Music Copyright Association. Suga has been credited as a writer and producer for BTS since 2014 and he released his first solo mixtape in 2016, *Agust D*. Produced entirely by Suga, the mixtape gave him the opportunity to tell his story. He speaks freely about his issues with obsessive compulsive disorder and depression and of his visits to psychiatrists.

"I really want to say that everyone in the world is lonely and everyone is sad […] say things are hard when they're hard."

When asked how he would describe himself, he said, "Min Suga. Genius. These two words should be enough." His dry sense of humor is loved because it's different from the other members. Another favorite moment was when Suga practiced his pick-up line: "You know BTS?"

Suga does not declare his love for ARMY in the same way as the other members, but he still shows appreciation. During a fan signing event in 2014, he told ARMY that when he made enough money he would buy them meat. When he was asked again a year later, he promised he would on March 9, 2018, his birthday. Not to let his fans down, on the day, he donated Korean beef to 39 orphanages in the name of ARMY. When BTS were preparing for their speech at the United Nations in 2018, Suga took the opportunity to praise their loyal fans.

"I don't think our acting alone is a big help to others. I think what's really amazing is the fact that the people who like us and support us are taking up [the cause] in that way."

STYLE FILE

Suga's style is relaxed – he likes to keep it comfortable and is often seen wearing oversized, cozy clothes. He once admitted in an interview that he first paid attention to fashion when he was 15, but he doesn't care much about it these days.

Staying true to his relaxed personality, Suga sticks to a muted color palette and wears a lot of black. He loves to wear black hats, from beanies and baseball caps to snapbacks and bucket hats. Suga is careful about the accessories that he picks to accompany his outfit – "Earrings, necklaces, bracelets, rings – I like them all."

♥ ♥ ♥ ♥ ♥ ♥ ♥

What do the boys say about Suga?

V:
"He really has a lot of knowledge."

Jin:
"He likes being attached to his bed!"

QUICK QUESTION

During BTS's third anniversary celebration, what did Suga announce as his special skill?

Answer: Lying down

33

CHAPTER FIVE:
Conquering the World

BTS have pushed boundaries ever since they dropped on to the music scene and they haven't stopped breaking records, accepting awards and collaborating with some of the hottest artists around. Here are just some of their best moments over the years.

RECORDS

★ In 2016, *Wings* became the year's highest-selling album on the Gaon charts (in South Korea) and "Blood, Sweat & Tears" achieved the "all-kill," topping all eight Korean music charts, as well as ranking number one on the iTunes charts in 23 countries. *Wings* also became the first Korean album to enter the Official Album Charts in the UK, coming in at number 62. BTS climbed even higher when their album *Love Yourself: Tear* entered at number eight in 2018.

★ Their single "Spring Day" was another all-kill, and reached number eight on the US iTunes chart, making BTS the first-ever K-pop band to break into the top ten.

★ They became the first Korean group to perform at the American Music Awards in 2017 with the legendary "DNA."

★ As of September 2017, BTS officially hold the world record for most Twitter engagements and, more specifically, the most Twitter engagements for a music group. At the time of the Guinness World Records announcement, BTS had amassed an average of 252,200 retweets per tweet on Twitter.

★ They became the first Korean group to have a song certified gold by the Recording Industry Association of America (RIAA) with "MIC Drop," which has since been certified platinum.

★ According to the Gaon album chart, *Love Yourself: Her* became the first album in 16 years to sell over 1.2 million copies in the first month of release.

★ They became the first-ever Korean artist to grab the No. 1 spot on the Billboard 200 in the US with *Love Yourself: Tear*. If that wasn't an achievement in itself, it was the first primarily foreign language album to reach No. 1 on the chart in 12 years.

★ When *Love Yourself: Tear* was released, it sold over 1 million units in its first week; a new record on the Hanteo Chart as they are the first artist to do so since the chart began in 1993.

★ BTS's "Fake Love" was the fastest music video to reach 10 million views on YouTube in 4 hours and 55 minutes.

QUICK QUESTION

What video previously held the record of the fastest music video to reach 10 million views?

AWARDS

★ "Best New Artist" – 2013 Melon Music Awards.

★ "New Rising Star" – 2014 Golden Disc Awards.

★ "Best New Artist" – 2014 Seoul Music Awards.

★ "Best Worldwide Performer" – 2015 Mnet Asian Music Awards.

★ "Best Album" for *The Most Beautiful Moment in Life: Young Forever* – 2016 Melon Music Awards.

★ "Artist of the Year" – 2016, 2017, 2018 Mnet Asian Music Awards.

★ "Top Social Artist" – Billboard Music Awards two years in a row for 2017 and 2018.

★ "Musician of the Year" – 2017 Korean Music Awards.

★ "Artist of the Year" – 2018 Korean Music Awards, becoming the first idol group to win.

★ The fifth-class "Hwagwan Order of Cultural Merit" – 2018 Korean Popular Culture & Arts Awards. They became the youngest recipients in history to receive this award.

★ "Biggest Fans" – 2018 MTV European Music Awards.

COLLABORATIONS

★ BTS's "Best of Me" produced by The Chainsmokers' Andrew Taggart
This track on BTS's *Love Yourself: Her* album came out of the boys meeting The Chainsmokers at the Billboard Music Awards in 2017.

★ BTS's "MIC Drop (Remix)" with Steve Aoki
This track was remixed by American DJ Steve Aoki on *Love Yourself: Her*. The song was inspired by former US president Barack Obama's mic drop.

★ BTS's "Idol" featuring Nicki Minaj
BTS released two versions of this single on the digital version of *Love Yourself: Answer*, one featuring Nicki Minaj guesting on vocals. They also released a second version of the music video which had an appearance from the Queen of Rap herself.

★ Steve Aoki's "Waste It On Me" featuring BTS
This ambient EDM track from Steve Aoki features BTS singing entirely in English for the first time (primarily performed by Jungkook and RM). It was part of Steve Aoki's *Neon Future III* album and earned BTS their first top ten on the electronic dance charts.

J-HOPE

Name:
Jung Hoseok

Also known as:
J-Hope, Hobi, Horse, Smile Hoya

Date of birth:
February 18, 1994

Star sign:
Aquarius

Birthplace:
Gwangju, South Korea

Height:
5'10"

Education:
Ilgok Middle School,
Kukje High School,
Global Cyber University

Languages:
Korean, basic English,
basic Japanese

Early career:
Studied at a famous dance
academy in Gwangju and was
a member of Neuron, a street
dance crew

Joined BTS:
2010

J-Hope is BTS's ray of sunshine. With his beaming smile and playful personality, he creates good energy that has a positive impact on the group.

Before J-Hope joined BTS, he was part of a street-dance team called Neuron. Dancing has always been a big part of his life. At the age of 14, J-Hope won a national dance competition in South Korea.

"I did a lot of popping and won a lot of prizes."

Forget money and fame, J-Hope is interested in inspiring and giving hope to fans. J-Hope wants people to get good vibes from listening to BTS and feel represented by the music.

"It would be hugely meaningful for me if I can become, like my namesake, hope for someone in the world."

J-Hope's desire to give hope to fans was shown in 2018, when he released his debut solo mixtape called *Hope World*. He called it his "calling card" to the world.

Jung Hoseok's positive attitude led him to choose the stage name "J-Hope." He wanted to be a source of hope and light for fans.

"My name has the deepest meaning out of all the others in the group. I put 'hope' in my name to be a hopeful existence in the group. I got J from my last name, Jung. That's how I became J-Hope."

Before joining Big Hit Entertainment, J-Hope auditioned at rival company JYP Entertainment. He was unsuccessful but he continued to practice dance, and it was this love of dance and willingness to work hard that caught the attention of Big Hit Entertainment. In December 2010, J-Hope became the third of the final BTS line-up to sign with Big Hit Entertainment and joined the group as an accomplished dancer.

J-Hope is one of the main dancers in BTS and often takes the lead in rehearsals. He works hard in the studio and has been credited for his part in creating and interpreting BTS's complex choreography. He has a level of enthusiasm and dedication like no other member, and he brings this passion to every performance. It's hard to forget his amazing dance skills in the Mnet Asian Music Awards (MAMA) battles in 2014 and 2015.

His love of dance inspired his VLive series "Hope on the Street." The videos feature J-Hope dancing and giving dance tips to viewers. These dance tips are also useful in the studio, and J-Hope is often found helping the other members tweak their routines. When discussing the choreography for dance breaks in *We Are Bulletproof Pt. 2*, he's said to have worked hard to fill the gaps that some of the other boys lack when dancing.

Alongside his moves, J-Hope was originally recruited as one of the vocal line. It wasn't until V joined the company six months later as a vocalist that J-Hope switched to the rap line. His original focus on vocal explains his smooth rapping technique, and when he sings in "Mama" it's clear to see why he was originally picked for a vocal role.

J-Hope's warm personality means that he gets along effortlessly with the rest of the group. His close relationship with his roommate Jimin is special and J-Hope has expressed how grateful he is that they have each other. He also has a lot of friends in the K-pop world, including Ravi from VIXX, Hyerin from EXID and Jo Kwon from 2PM. 2PM's leader, Jo, and J-Hope have been friends since before BTS's debut and they have supported each other ever since. When J-Hope was still a trainee in 2012, he featured as a rapper on Jo's solo track "Animal."

In 2018, J-Hope became the third member of the group to put out an individual mixtape, following leader RM's first mixtape in 2015 and Suga's *Agust D* release in 2016.

"I have been and continue to be deeply influenced by them [RM and Suga], from the day we began to where we are today, and I always thought it was awesome that they were telling their own personal stories and making music in their own styles."

J-Hope's mixtape features seven tracks that span pop, tropical, trap, EDM and rap, and his warmth radiates throughout. The mixtape, aptly named *Hope World*, delves into J-Hope's personal reflections on fame and success with instantly catchy beats. It soared in the charts as he became the highest-charting K-pop solo act on the Billboard 200.

STYLE FILE

J-Hope's style is perhaps the most exciting of the BTS boys. Sometimes he's casual in a bomber jacket and other times he's in a sparkly suit. But whatever J-Hope wears, he puts in maximum effort and looks super stylish. He's not afraid of a strong pattern or print, and wears whatever he wants, whether anyone thinks it works or not. He's most comfortable wearing shorts, oversized coats and one of his many hats, with his "acorn" pouch and his notorious Balenciaga trainers. His look is often finished with a pair of round, thin wire-framed glasses, and of course his signature beaming smile.

♥ ♥ ♥ ♥ ♥ ♥ ♥

What do the boys say about J-Hope?

Jimin:
"J-Hope is a bright guy, laughs a lot and has become hopeful like his name."

RM:
"He's good at mixing with others and with the rest of the group."

QUICK QUESTION
What is J-Hope's biggest fear?

Answer: Snakes – J-Hope once screamed "I hate snaku!"

CHAPTER SIX:
Behind the Scenes

If watching their music videos or following them on social media isn't enough to get a daily dose of the boys, BTS release content that takes fans behind the scenes.

VLIVE

This South Korean live video streaming service allows celebrities to broadcast on the internet. BTS can connect directly with fans through their channel, which features series such as *Run BTS!*, *BTS Gayo* and *Bon Voyage*. The channel currently has over 11 million subscribers and has over 550 videos for fans to access.

Where to find this?
All videos can be found on VLIVE.TV and the VLIVE app. Some of the videos require a subscription and payment to access the content.

Run BTS!

This variety show began on August 1, 2015, and consists of episodes of BTS facing challenges, doing activities and having a lot of fun. After their 50th episode in April 2018, BTS revealed that the most-viewed episode was EP31 (featuring the "kung kung tta" word chain game), followed closely by EP11 (the school skit) and EP20 (the cook-off).

Where to find this?
All videos can be found on VLIVE.TV and the VLIVE app.

BTS Gayo

This variety show began on August 11, 2015, and is a musical game show where the band are the contestants each week. There have been 15 "tracks" to date where the boys compete against each other on different aspects of K-pop culture.

Where to find this?
All videos can be found on VLIVE.TV and the VLIVE app.

Bon Voyage

This eight-episode-per-season reality show follows BTS's travels around the world. There have been three seasons so far with one airing each year since 2016. In season one, BTS explored Scandinavia, the second season took place in Hawaii and the third season in Malta.

Where to find this?
The episodes can be found on VLIVE.TV and the VLIVE app. Each episode requires a subscription and payment to access the content.

Rookie King: Channel Bangtan

This eight-episode series began at the start of BTS, with the first episode airing September 3, 2013, and finishing October 22, 2013. This was one of the first insights into the silliness of the band's relationships as they are featured cooking, bowling and playing games together.

Where to find this?
You can find episodes with English subtitles on YouTube.

Bangtan Bombs

These are short videos uploaded by Big Hit Entertainment which show the boys messing around. There are over 455 videos to choose from and they can range from two seconds to up to ten minutes in length. The first "bomb" was posted on June 19, 2013, and featured Jungkook filming Jimin, and in the top right-hand corner was a logo of a cartoon BTS bomb.

Where to find this?
The "Bangtan Bomb" playlist on the BANGTANTV YouTube channel.

Festa

This two-week celebration occurs each year, beginning June 1 on the anniversary of their 2013 debut. The content is not always the same, but fans always enjoy a video of the boys celebrating their birthday. There is also a live Home Party event which takes place in South Korea. Tickets can only be purchased by certain fans, but it can be watched online for free.

Where to find this?
On all social media accounts including the BANGTANTV YouTube channel. The full-length 105-minute video for Home Party can be viewed on VLIVE.TV.

Muster

This annual event – part concert, part variety show – takes place in Seoul, South Korea. BTS call their yearly fan meetings "musters," which means an assembly of troops – fitting, as their fans are called ARMY.

Where to find this?
Recordings of the events are available to purchase on DVD. It usually contains several discs, including behind-the-scenes footage, as well as stickers, photocards and a photobook.

JIMIN

Name:
Park Jimin

Also known as:
Jimin, Jiminie, Mochi,
Chim Chim

Date of birth:
October 13, 1995

Star sign:
Libra

Birthplace:
Busan, South Korea

Height:
5'8"

Education:
Heodang Elementary School,
Yoonsan Middle School,
Busan High School of Arts,
Korean Arts High School,
Global Cyber University

Languages:
Korean

Early career:
Modern dance student

Joined BTS:
2012

Jimin was the last member to join BTS and was brought in just months before the line-up was confirmed.

Before Jimin joined BTS, he was studying at the Busan High School of Arts, where he showed a great deal of natural talent. His teachers were so impressed that they encouraged him to audition for Big Hit Entertainment.

"It was my first ever audition so my hands were shaking a lot when I opened the door, but because I started dancing at a young age, I danced very confidently."

When he first joined BTS he was asked to rap, but he soon discovered that his talents did not extend that far.

"After they had me rap once, they were like, 'Let's just work harder on vocals.'"

Jimin works very hard to be the best band member that he can be. He is conscious of how hard the other boys work and strives to do well in every performance.

Jimin was invited to become an apprentice at Big Hit Entertainment, during which time he performed as a backing dancer for a stage performance of Glam's "Glamorous" and also appeared in a video clip for "Party (XXO)."

As a trainee, Jimin focused on his singing and dancing. He often worked so hard he only had three hours' sleep at night. This was an incredible level of dedication, as he was also studying at school. Jimin was so eager to improve, that it's been said his motto is, "Let's keep trying until we can't anymore."

In the BTS documentary *Burn the Stage*, Jimin spoke about how this level of commitment can go too far. He admitted that he thinks of himself as a perfectionist and dwells on the smallest mistakes on stage because he feels he has let the other members down.

He is truly at the heart of BTS and he's always there with a helping hand if one of the members is struggling. The boys have often confessed that Jimin is the one they turn to if they need comfort. It's easy for Jimin to empathize with them and offer advice as he draws from his own vulnerabilities. He has struggled with bullying and his appearance, especially with his weight. In the past, he often skipped meals to lose weight and didn't look after himself. Thankfully, he now follows a healthy diet and exercise routine, and takes pride in himself.

Although in the early years he was known for showing off his amazing abs on stage, Jimin is actually very shy. He enjoys wearing make-up, especially eyeliner, and confessed it's his secret weapon. As an introvert, the make-up helps him put on a front on stage. Jimin does come alive when he performs, and some of the other boys even joke that in the live shows he hogs the center stage!

"When I don't wear eyeliner, I am shy and I feel like I can't dance."

Like all the other boys, Jimin uses music to express his feelings. This can be seen on the solo track "Lie," from *Wings*. It is a beautiful song about insecurities, self-doubt and the intense pressure of being a perfectionist. He has a passion for connecting with his fans and helping them work on their own anxieties.

"It would be really great if our music continues to touch people. Once your heart is moved, it will develop into something better and positive."

Jimin's connection with his fans extends beyond the music, and he frequently posts to BTS social media accounts, updating ARMY with plenty of messages, photos and videos. This interaction has meant that his relationship with his fans has blossomed over the years. His "selca" (selfie) obsession means that fans receive plenty of pictures of Jimin looking super-cute, and his posts collect thousands of likes, shares and comments. Among many fans, Jimin is known as the group's "recruiting fairy," because he attracts so many new fans. As ARMY sometimes say, "Once you Jimin, you can't Jimout!"

So it's not surprising that Jimin won the monthly *Peeper x Billboard* Award for "Top K-Pop Artist – Individual" from January to May 2018. *Peeper x Billboard* is a collaboration between the social media app Peeper and Billboard Korea. This award is voted for by fans and his prize was donated to UNICEF in his name.

STYLE FILE

All the boys rock the boy-next-door look, but Jimin does it the best. Whether he is traveling around the world or chilling in the dorm, all of Jimin's looks are modest yet fashionable.

He's often seen wearing a simple T-shirt, ripped jeans and a leather jacket. Accessories really pull Jimin's style together – whether it's a designer bag or a stunning dangly earring. There's clearly a lot of thought behind his look.

What do the boys say about Jimin?

Suga:
"He puts in the effort to try his hardest."

V:
"He's cute, kind and a friend who is trustworthy."

QUICK QUESTION

According to Jimin, what are his three requirements for happiness?

Answer: Love, money, stage

CHAPTER SEVEN:
Challenging the Status Quo

BTS are known for tackling important social issues. Standing up and speaking out for what is right is at the core of BTS's values.

The boys write a lot of their own songs, using them to describe the pressures in many young people's lives. BTS's very first single, "No More Dream," tells fans to follow their own dreams rather than do what society expects. The key lyric reminds listeners, "Even if you live for a day/ Do something/Put away your weakness." This theme appears on 2016's "Not Today," an anthem "for all the underdogs," and 2018's "Paradise."

BTS's drive to comment on politics is clear in "Silver Spoon" (aka "Baepsae") where they address the "cursed" generation. RM raps, "Thanks to those that came before us I'm spread too thin." This resonates with generations worldwide who feel the pinch of a lack of money or opportunities.

RM criticizes political apathy in "Am I Wrong," with "If what you see on the news is nothing to you, you're not normal, you're abnormal."

GIVING BACK

"Spring Day" includes the phrase "Mayday, Mayday." This might be a reference to the 2014 South Korean Sewol ferry tragedy which resulted in the death of over 300 passengers, mostly high school students. This tragedy hit BTS hard and, along with Big Hit Entertainment, they donated 100 million KRW (roughly 68,000 GBP/85,000 US dollars) to the Sewol Ferry Disaster Family Council.

PARTNERSHIPS

After releasing their *Love Yourself: Her* album in 2017, BTS announced a partnership with the United Nations International Children's Emergency Fund (UNICEF) for a cause close to their hearts. They staged the campaign "LOVE MYSELF" as part of the larger global #ENDviolence campaign to prevent young people having to live in fear of violence. Along with Big Hit Entertainment, they pledged 500 million KRW (roughly 340,000 GBP/440,000 US dollars) to UNICEF, plus three percent of the physical album sales profit from the *Love Yourself* trilogy and donations of all income from the sales of official goods.

Since their debut, BTS have wanted to spread the word about the importance of loving yourself to young people who have lost faith and are in pain. It was announced on November 2, 2018, that the *Love Yourself* initiative had raised over 1 million US dollars for UNICEF.

SPEAKING OUT

In September 2018, RM gave a powerful speech on behalf of BTS at the United Nations (UN). He spoke about his insecurities surrounding his self-worth and urged others to know their value. It was a historic moment as it was the first time a K-pop band had addressed the UN. As the speech went viral, the themes harked back to older songs before the *Love Yourself* albums. In "Cypher Pt.4" from *Wings*, the line "I love, I love, I love myself / I know, I know, I know myself" influenced and taught young people to consider what self-love means.

As RM finished his speech at the UN, he said, "What is your name? Speak yourself." He reminds us that BTS do not have all the answers and they too go through hard times, but in those hard times they reach out and invite fans to find a way through it together.

Name:
Kim Taehyung

Also known as:
V, Taetae, Human Gucci, Vante

Date of birth:
December 30, 1995

Star sign:
Capricorn

Birthplace:
Daegu, South Korea

Height:
5'10"

Education:
Changnam Elementary School,
Geochang Middle School,
Daegu First High School,
Korean Arts High School,
Global Cyber University

Languages:
Korean, Japanese

Early career:
Saxophone player

Joined BTS:
2012

V may be the second-youngest member of the group, but he has been named the most fashionable in the group.

V is often described as a family man. He had a very happy childhood and is extremely close to his family. Growing up in a family of farmers isn't the most traditional route to a pop career, but V had always wanted to be a singer.

"Don't be trapped in someone else's dream."

V's father once said that a singer should play at least one instrument, so V learned how to play the saxophone. He worked hard and won first prize at a regional competition.

"There was a time I wanted to be a saxophone player rather than a singer."

V showcased his saxophone skills in 2016 when he played on the South Korean variety television show, *Star Show 360*. It was his first time playing in seven years so was a little rusty at first, but soon began to bust out some tunes.

V had his eye on becoming an idol and joined a dance academy as a teenager. Big Hit Entertainment were holding auditions in his town, so V accompanied a friend. Although V did not intend to audition, he was spotted by one of the rookie development team who convinced him to give it a go. Once he had permission from his parents, he jumped on stage and danced, rapped and even told some great jokes. He was snapped up straight away and was the only successful applicant of the day!

Like Jimin, V went through a rigorous apprenticeship program. He gained experience by appearing in videos for other Big Hit Entertainment artists while he prepared for stardom. Before his debut, V picked his stage name from three potential choices – the other two were Six and Lex.

"The members all said that V fit me best, so I picked V to stand for Victory."

V was BTS's secret weapon and his membership was kept under wraps until just before debut. There were no photos or videos of V to tease fans, and even when he was at BTS's pre-debut events, such as RM and Jungkook's graduations, he was kept out of shot. It was hard for V to be left in the corner and sit by himself, but once he was revealed, it was worth the wait. V was an immediate hit with fans.

On stage, V is professional and sophisticated, but off-stage he can be quite silly and is often in a world of his own. He was once caught speaking a made-up language. To stop himself getting bored while doing his chores he would sometimes act out little plays, playing all the different parts.

Along with his dancing and singing, V is an accomplished actor. He landed a supporting role, as Suk Han-sung, in the 2016 KBS2 historical drama *Hwarang: The Poet Warrior Youth*. It focused on the lives and loves of a group of young men in Korea over 2,000 years ago. He gave a beautiful performance and his acting was commended.

His interaction with the acting world has meant that V has plenty of friends outside of BTS. He is very popular and is regularly pictured with celebrities and idols, most notably BTOB's Sungjae, singer Jang Moonbok and Block B's Park Kyung.

Outside of music and acting, V remains creative and has a love for art. When BTS were on tour in America, he took any opportunity to experience the art and culture on offer.

"Every one of the shows on the US tour was unforgettable. Personally, my favorite moment was when I went to MoMA [Museum of Modern Art] in New York, and the Art Institute of Chicago."

V loves to talk about the future and most of the conversations surround his family. In 2016, V said what he would like to do most in the future is to buy his parents a big apartment and a new car. He even knows the names of his future children, admitting he would love a boy called Taekwon and a girl called Taegeuk. He wants to be a cool dad just like his own and to make his kids laugh all the time.

STYLE FILE

V does not follow the crowd when it comes to his fashion sense. His vibrant personality shows through his outfits with his quirky but chic look. He combines various styles and has expensive taste.

Tigers and snakes have been a constant theme because V loves the brand Gucci – not just the clothes, but the accessories too. It's not surprising that he got the nickname Human Gucci!

What do the boys say about V?

RM:
"In my opinion, he's 10% genius and 90% idiot."

Jungkook:
"V always wants to do lots of things."

QUICK QUESTION
What is the name of V's dog?

Answer: Yeontan

TIMELINE

Take a look at some of BTS's greatest moments over the years.

2005

♥ Bang Si-hyuk sets up his own company, Big Hit Entertainment.

2010

♥ Bang Si-hyuk has the idea to launch a hip-hop idol group.

♥ RM, Suga and J-Hope audition and join Big Hit Entertainment as trainees.

2011

♥ Auditions for the group that will become BTS continue.

2012

♥ Jungkook, V, Jin and Jimin join and the group is complete.

♥ Bangtan Sonyeondan (BTS) is decided as the group's name.

♥ Big Hit Entertainment launches a blog to announce the arrival of BTS.

♥ December 17: The first video is added to their YouTube channel.

2018

♥ February 28: Become the first idol group to win the Korean Music Awards "Artist of the Year."

♥ May 27: BTS become the first K-pop group to have a number one album in the US with *Love Yourself: Tear*.

♥ June 28: Included in *TIME* magazine's list of 25 most influential people on the internet.

♥ September 28: First K-pop group to address the United Nations.

♥ November 4: First Korean artist to surpass 1 billion streams on Apple Music.

2017

♥ February 12: "Spring Day" reaches number eight on the US iTunes chart. BTS become the first-ever K-pop band to break into the top ten.

♥ May 20: Win "Top Social Artist" at the Billboard Music Awards.

♥ September 18: *Love Yourself: Her* is released and becomes the biggest-selling physical album for 16 years in Gaon chart history.

♥ November 20: Become the first Korean group to perform at the American Music Awards.

2013

♥ **June 11:** First music video, "No More Dream," is released.

♥ **June 12:** BTS's debut showcase takes place. Their first album, *2 Cool 4 Skool*, is released.

♥ **June 13:** Perform live for the first time on *M Countdown* and *Music Bank*.

♥ **June 19:** First "Bangtan Bomb" streams on their YouTube channel.

2014

♥ **January 1:** Win "New Rising Star" award at the Golden Disc Awards.

♥ **March 1:** *Skool Luv Affair* enters the Billboard World Albums chart for the first time at number three.

♥ **April 1:** Make their TV variety show debut on *Beatles Code*.

♥ **October 17–19:** Their first ever solo full-length concert, "The Red Bullet," sells out in five minutes.

☆
☆
☆
☆
☆

2016

♥ *Bon Voyage* streams on VLIVE over the summer.

♥ **October 9:** "Blood, Sweat & Tears" achieves the "all-kill," topping all eight Korean music charts, as well as ranking number one on the iTunes charts in 23 countries.

♥ **October 14:** *Wings* becomes the first Korean album to enter the Official Album Charts in the United Kingdom, coming in at number 62.

♥ **November 19:** *The Most Beautiful Moment in Life: Young Forever* wins best album at the Melon Music Awards; their first **Daesang**.

2015

♥ **May 5:** Win their first music show at the 27th *The Show Choice*.

♥ *BTS Bokbulbok*, *BTS Gayo* and *Run BTS!* stream on VLIVE over the summer.

♥ **October 26:** Puma announces an endorsement deal with BTS.

♥ **November 30:** Become the first K-pop act that are not under YG Entertainment or SM Entertainment to enter the Billboard 200 with *The Most Beautiful Moment in Life Pt. 2*.

♥   ♥   ♥   ♥   ♥   ♥   ♥

A **Daesang** is the prestigious "Grand Prize" at a music award show, awarded for the artist, song or album of the year.

♥   ♥   ♥   ♥   ♥   ♥   ♥

JUNGKOOK

Name:
Jeon Jungkook

Also known as:
Jungkook, Jungkookie,
JK, Bunny

Date of birth:
September 1, 1997

Star sign:
Virgo

Birthplace:
Busan, South Korea

Height:
5'10"

Education:
Baekyang Middle School,
Shingu Middle School,
School of Performance
Arts High School

Languages:
Korean, basic English,
basic Japanese

Early career:
Auditioned for South Korean
talent show *Superstar K*

Joined BTS:
2012

Jungkook was only 15 when BTS first hit the scene and he postponed starting high school because he was so busy with the band.

He had always dreamed of becoming a singer and, before BTS debuted, he spent time in America working on his singing and dance moves.

"Effort makes you. You will regret someday if you don't do your best now."

By the time he auditioned for *Superstar K* (a talent show in South Korea), he was on the radar of plenty of huge entertainment companies, including Big Hit Entertainment. Many people have asked why he chose Big Hit. Jungkook has spoken about idolizing RM from the beginning — he had seen RM rapping and decided there and then.

"I thought RM was so cool, so I wanted to sign with them."

Jungkook and RM performed together on an original song in 2016. The track, "I Know," was made for BTS's debut anniversary celebration, Festa. The song thanks fans for standing by the group over the years.

Jungkook discovered music at a young age. He was inspired to try singing and street dance, and joined a local breakdance club. But when he arrived as a trainee at the age of 13, he did not have enough experience to match the other boys. He recalls the time when Bang Si-hyuk told him that there was no emotion in his dancing.

Instead of packing up and going home, he worked harder. Big Hit Entertainment booked him on to an intensive street-dance course at the famous dance academy Movement Lifestyle in Los Angeles. Although he found it tough, he learned a lot and by the end of 2012, he was revealed as the sixth member of BTS. It was a gamble allowing him to debut as he was so young and lacking in confidence, but the boys rallied around him in support.

Jungkook is the **maknae** (youngest) of the group. He often reflects on how he came of age as a member of the band. BTS are a family to him and each of them has influenced who he has become as a man.

"The guys filled me in one by one. They put the scattered pieces of my puzzle back together."

He is sometimes referred to as the Golden Maknae because he's good at singing, dancing, rapping and sports. Jungkook is easily the most athletic member of the group. He's a fantastic dancer, great at running and he's also a super-strong wrestler. He's so strong that he can lift up any of his bandmates!

A self-proclaimed Belieber, Jungkook would love to collaborate with Justin Bieber in the future. He's getting in plenty of practice covering lots of his songs like "Purpose," "Nothing Like Us" and "Boyfriend." All his covers can be found on YouTube.

As the least-confident member of the group, it's not surprising that he engages the least with fans on social media. ARMY have tried to encourage him to post more, but it does not come as naturally to him as it does to the other boys. However, he understands how important ARMY are and has been trying to use social media more to connect with them.

"We do our best and keep working, no matter what. Our fans have supported us so much and we have to go even higher from here. Our international success has made me want to create better music, and that's why we all try to listen and study more music."

Jungkook is very sensitive if he feels he has let ARMY down. When BTS made their live debut in the UK in 2018, Jungkook broke down on stage after injuring his heel during warm-up, leaving him unable to dance. He sat on a stool for most of the gig which was upsetting for him as one of the strongest dancers of the group. He later confessed to blaming himself and struggling to focus — he felt sorry for the fans who had attended the concert.

♥   ♥   ♥   ♥   ♥   ♥   ♥

The **maknae** is often the cutest and most playful member of the group, and receives the most attention from the others.

♥   ♥   ♥   ♥   ♥   ♥   ♥

STYLE FILE

Jungkook knows what he likes – a simple shirt and denim jeans suit him just fine. He's fond of hats, especially a beanie or bucket hat, but his favorite item of clothing is a plain white or black T-shirt.

Out of all the boys, Jungkook's style has changed the least over the years, but he's still learning and navigating his identity. Fans look forward to seeing his style develop in the years to come.

♥ ♥ ♥ ♥ ♥ ♥ ♥

What do the boys say about Jungkook?

RM:
"He's individualistic and doesn't share clothes."

V:
"Truthfully, he's the same as me!"

QUICK QUESTION

What did Jungkook aspire to be when he was growing up?

Answer: A professional badminton player.

ULTIMATE QUIZ

You've read about the boys and their journey to fame, so now it's time to put your knowledge to the test. Do you know BTS well enough to answer the 20 questions below? Give it a go and find out your true fan status by checking if your answers are correct on **page 61**.

1. What was the name of RM's first rap crew?

....

♥

2. What is their song "Paldogangsan" often known as?

....

♥

3. How many online votes won them the "Top Social Artist" award at the 2017 BBMAs?

....

♥

4. What did Jin dress up as for the "Halloween War of Hormone" dance practice?

....

♥

5. What was their first ever full-length solo concert called?

....

♥

6. What was V's songwriting debut?

....

♥

7. What is J-Hope's favorite book from childhood?

....

♥

8. Which Korean pop superstar inspired Jimin to become an idol?

....

♥

9. Which album saw them become the first Korean act to break into the UK charts?

....

10. What baked goods does Jungkook want to eat in an early Bangtan Bomb?

....

♥

11. What historical Korean drama did V star in?

....

♥

12. Which four Justin Bieber songs has Jungkook posted videos of himself covering?

....

♥

13. What day did RM record his first all-English video log?

....

♥

14. In 2013, BTS did an interview in an unusually decorated room. What covered the walls?

....

♥

15. What figurines decorated Jimin's 19th birthday cake?

....

♥

16. What musical instrument did Jimin once draw for Suga?

....

♥

17. Which of their songs samples a song by Grammy Award winning Keb' Mo'?

....

♥

18. What is the English translation of the name of Suga's mother's restaurant?

....

♥

19. What is the name of J-Hope's sister Dawon's clothing line?

....

♥

20. What is the name of the Big Hit Performance Director who choreographed "Fake Love"?

....

CHAPTER EIGHT:
The Future

BTS have been breaking records left and right, with no signs of slowing down anytime soon. The future is certainly looking bright for these boys.

In 2018, BTS released three albums (two Korean and one Japanese), toured the world, produced a third season of their travel reality show (*Bon Voyage*) and won many historic awards. With their contract coming to an end in 2019, it seemed like perhaps BTS were making their mark on the world before their final farewell.

> **"We know that popularity is not forever, so we enjoy the ride, the roller coaster, and when it ends, it just finishes."**
> – RM in 2018

In South Korea, all able-bodied men are expected to serve a period of around two years in the military. Fans were anxious that this would be the cause of a break-up. But these worries were quashed on October 17, 2018, when Big Hit Entertainment announced that the boys had re-signed for another seven years. In their statement they said, "with Big Hit Entertainment's support, we'll continue to strive to give our best for fans all around the world." ARMY were overjoyed and landed #7MoreYearsOfBTS atop Twitter's Worldwide trends list. With BTS now on the scene until 2026, the world is hungry with anticipation of what the future holds.

Tipped as the "exclusive BTS story," a documentary film following BTS's 2017 "Wings" tour had a worldwide cinematic release on November 15, 2018. The film pulled in 18.5 million US dollars at the box office following its second limited run on the weekend of December 5. Both the original and follow-up runs drew 2 million viewers to cinemas worldwide.

As part of their sold-out *Love Yourself* world tour, they made history stateside in October 2018 with a sold-out show at Citi Field as they became the first Korean act to hold a solo stadium-sized concert in the US. They also performed in Canada, the UK, Europe, Japan and Taiwan and continued touring in 2019 in Singapore, Hong Kong and Thailand.

WHAT NEXT?

Suga hasn't been too shy to announce that his next goal is to win a Grammy. This is awarded by and to artists for technical achievement, not sales or chart positions. He dreams of playing the Super Bowl half-time show with 71,000 people in the stadium and 120 million watching on the television. This might have seemed out of reach for BTS a few years ago, but recent events have shown that they are capable of anything they set their minds to.

ULTIMATE QUIZ: THE ANSWERS

1. DaeNamHyup or DNH
2. "Satoori Rap"
3. 300 million
4. Jack Sparrow
5. The Red Bullet
6. "Hold Me Tight"
7. *Twenty Thousand Leagues Under the Sea*
8. Rain
9. *Wings*
10. Doughnuts
11. *Hwarang: The Poet Warrior Youth*
12. "Boyfriend," "Nothing Like Us," "Purpose" and "2U"
13. March 26, 2013
14. Post-it Notes
15. Teddy bears
16. A piano
17. "Am I Wrong"
18. Big Hearted Grandma's Blood Sausage Soup
19. Mejiwoo
20. Son Sungdeuk